*Growing*
**GREEN**

# ORGANIC FOODS

### by David M. Barker

LERNER PUBLICATIONS · MINNEAPOLIS

Content Consultant: Courtney Baines Smith, Department of
Sustainable Development, Appalachian State University, Boone, North Carolina

Lerner Publications Company
A division of Lerner Publishing Group, Inc.
241 First Avenue North
Minneapolis, MN 55401 USA

For reading levels and more information, look up this title at
www.lernerbooks.com.

**Library of Congress Cataloging-in-Publication Data**

Barker, David, 1959-
 Organic foods / by David M. Barker.
    pages cm.—(Growing green)
 Includes bibliographical references and index.
 Audience: Ages 11-14.
 Audience: Grades 7-8.
 ISBN 978-1-4677-9391-9 (lb : alk. paper)—ISBN 978-1-4677-9712-2 (eb pdf)
 1. Organic farming—Juvenile literature. 2. Natural foods—Juvenile literature. I. Title.
 S605.5.B366 2016
 631.5'84—dc23
                        2015027079

Manufactured in the United States of America
1 – VP – 12/31/15

Table of

# CONTENTS

# WHAT IS "ORGANIC"?

There is a growing organic food trend sweeping the nation, and many grocery stores feature a variety of foods labeled *organic*. In these organic sections, you will find carrots, onions, kale, bananas, and oranges—almost everything found in the rest of the produce department. At the butcher counter there's also organic beef, chicken, and pork. The dairy cooler holds organic milk, cheese, yogurt, and eggs.

Organic food is available in many areas across the United States and in many other countries around the world. Why is it so in demand? One reason is that organic foods are not exposed to human-made pesticides and fertilizers. But that's not the whole story. Farmers who grow organic products, and the people who buy them, also want agriculture to be sustainable. This means they want to grow food without using large amounts of energy and materials and to allow farmers, workers, and farm communities to maintain a fair standard of living. Avoiding the use of chemicals is just one part of a trend toward sustainable agriculture.

Have you noticed the organic foods section at your local grocery store?

# FIND ORGANIC FOOD NEAR YOU

Is there a farmers' market near you? Farmers' markets are one of the best places to find organic foods. Farmers' markets are usually open once a week or on weekends, since the farmers need to be farming the rest of the week. They are often located in a central building, or on an outside lot if the weather is nice. Farmers bring their vegetables, fruits, and meats. Sometimes they also sell baked goods and prepared foods such as preserves, maple syrup, or sauces. Don't be discouraged if you live in a large city. Even large cities have farmers' markets and urban farms—farms of varying sizes that are in or near the city. Urban farming is a growing trend, and a lot of these farms are organic. Visit your local farmers' market or one of the farms on your own, or suggest it as a class trip!

## What Is Sustainable?

What is the difference between organic and sustainable farming? For something to be sustainable, it cannot use resources, such as soil, water, and nutrients, faster than they are renewed. A sustainable farm does its best to use only the sun's energy and the natural cycles of nutrients and water to grow crops instead of applying human-made pesticides and fertilizers. Using these methods, farmers can produce food without damaging the soil or the environment and continue producing food forever. Sustainable farms also allow the farmers, the people who work for them, and their economic communities to prosper.

# The Origins of Agriculture

For most of history, humans fed themselves by hunting animals and gathering plant foods. This changed approximately 12,000 years ago with one of the most important inventions ever: agriculture. It was invented in several parts of the world at the same time, including China, the Middle East, and Africa. Agriculture is the practice of breeding, planting, nurturing, and harvesting living organisms for food. These organisms include animals, plants, and fungi.

Humans soon learned to breed varieties of plants and animals that fit their local climate and taste. Another important skill was being able to use

This wall painting from Egypt dates back to 1200 BCE. It shows an ancient Egyptian using domesticated livestock to pull a plow.

the same soil for crops year after year. When crops grow, they pull nutrients, especially nitrogen, from the soil. If humans harvest the crops, the nutrients are not returned to the soil for the next crop to use. Also, some methods of agriculture can cause soil to wash away, which makes it increasingly difficult to grow crops. One solution to these problems is crop rotation.

With crop rotation, the kind of crop grown in a field is changed each year. In some years the field may be left fallow, meaning no crops are grown. Crop rotation works best when one of the crops is a legume, such as beans or clover for animal feed. Unlike other crops, legumes cooperate with bacteria to capture nitrogen from the air and add it to the soil. This nitrogen stays in the soil and feeds the next crops planted in the field. Over time, people found other ways of enriching the soil, including adding nutrients back in the form of a fertilizer, such as animal manure. Finally, farmers learned how to collect and direct water in climates where rainfall was scarce.

# The Agricultural Revolution

In the late 1700s and the 1800s in the United Kingdom, food production by agriculture greatly increased thanks to a new crop rotation method. The method rotated crops in four different fields each year. The crops were rye grass, barley or oats, and turnips, a new crop that could be fed to livestock. Unlike in previous methods, fields were never left fallow, so production increased without using up soil nutrients. Meanwhile, better breeding improved crops and livestock. New types of plows made plowing faster and easier. And new types of fertilizers added nutrients to the soil. The increase in food allowed for a large population increase in the

Leaving a field fallow allows nutrients to return to the soil, making it better for production the next season.

United Kingdom. These changes in farming were copied across the British Empire and Europe. Historians think the agricultural revolution allowed workers to participate in and fuel the Industrial Revolution. During the Industrial Revolution, which took place from the late 1700s to the early 1800s, manufacturing evolved and societies across Europe and the United States became more urban and industrialized.

Into the 1900s, farm production continued to improve. More trade and shipping of food increased agricultural profits. New machines replaced human workers. In 1909, Fritz Haber, a German chemist, invented a method

# FOUNDERS OF ORGANIC AGRICULTURE

Agriculturist Lord Northbourne (1896–1982) used biodynamic agriculture, which focuses on treating soil, plants, and livestock as one entity with spiritual, ethical, and ecological approaches. This organic farming method was developed in Germany. Lord Northbourne was responsible for first using the term *organic farming*, by which he meant that the farm itself was like a living organism.

English botanist Sir Albert Howard studied farming in India from 1905 to 1931. He is one of the important founders of organic and sustainable farming. He learned and improved methods of farming used by small farmers in India. Howard also wrote several popular books explaining organic farming methods. He wrote about creating healthy soil using compost, which uses bacteria and fungi to break down unused plant parts and animal manure into a natural fertilizer.

Howard's books influenced another English citizen, Lady Eve Balfour. She started the Haughley experiment in Suffolk, England. The experiment compared organic and nonorganic farming methods. Balfour believed farmers had become too reliant on artificial fertilizers. Her book *The Living Soil* was published in 1943, and she founded the Soil Association in 1946. The Soil Association still exists and promotes organic farming methods in the United Kingdom and around the world.

to pull nitrogen from the atmosphere and make artificial fertilizer. This method requires large amounts of energy, which the manufacturers got from coal and oil.

# The Green Revolution

During the twentieth century, human populations grew rapidly. Some countries around the world were not able to grow enough food, and their people faced famine. News of these deadly shortfalls spread quickly. There were concerns that the human population could grow larger than the planet's ability to feed us.

A visit to Mexico in 1940 led US Vice President Elect Henry Wallace to start a research program there to improve agricultural productivity. Wallace observed that in Mexico, farmers were very poor, soil was damaged, and crop yields were small compared to those in the United States. His research program brought together Mexican and international scientists to create a new corn variety that had greater yields. Yield is the amount of a crop that can be harvested from an area of land. Higher yields mean more food and more profit. The researchers then developed and bred wheat varieties that had far greater yields, but only when fields were irrigated and treated with artificial fertilizer.

This research started what has come to be known as the Green Revolution. The Green Revolution (1940s–1970s) produced a huge increase in crop yield and production in countries that previously had trouble growing enough food. It accomplished this increase with four main changes: the creation of new breeds of corn, wheat, and rice; the use of artificial fertilizers; the use of pesticides; and the combination of the new breeds with both fertilizers and pesticides.

The Green Revolution has been celebrated as a success because it appeared to prevent widespread famine despite the rapid increase in human population. But the increases came mainly from using fertilizer and pesticides, which means that farmers depend on outside suppliers and must spend large amounts of money to keep yields high even though the prices they receive for their crops are not increasing. Both fertilizers and pesticides require large amounts of energy to produce, which requires the burning of fossil fuels, thus contributing to atmospheric pollution and global climate change.

In the 1940s, researchers developed this higher-yielding variety of wheat, which is resistant to rust, a fungus that attacks wheat.

The Green Revolution helped to develop this higher-yield variety of corn, which grows well in Mexican soils.

# Conventional Farming and Sustainable Farming

All of these developments led to what is now described as conventional farming. Conventional farming involves a lot of different methods, but in general it means bringing a lot of outside material to the farm, including artificial fertilizers, pesticides, and special seeds developed and sold by large companies. It also means growing the same crop year after year on very large fields. Conventional farming of animals often involves keeping livestock inside for much of their lives. Instead of eating plants outdoors, the animals are given processed foods that contain growth hormones and low doses of antibiotics.

Sustainable and organic farming go back in history farther than most people realize. These methods have been used since ancient times because fertilizers and pesticides were not always available. But organic farming as we know it today is a reaction to many of the farming methods that came about during the agricultural and Green Revolutions.

## To Your HEALTH

## PESTICIDES IN THE FOOD CHAIN

Most compounds that dissolve fall into one of two groups—those that dissolve in water and those that dissolve in oils. Many pesticides belong to the second group, and this can cause serious problems. Chemicals that can dissolve in oil mix well with fat because fats are similar to oils. Animals store energy as fat. This means that animals store pesticides along with the fat. An animal that eats plants, such as a caterpillar, eats only small amounts of pesticide, but they build up in its body over time. The pesticide may not kill the caterpillar. However, many animals eat large numbers of caterpillars, ingesting large amounts of pesticides along with them. This chain continues to the next predator, with the pesticide getting more and more concentrated. This process is known as biomagnification. Biomagnification also applies to humans who eat large amounts of fish that have been exposed to pesticides. State and federal agencies set guidelines for how much fish to eat depending on who you are and where the fish come from. The guidelines are designed to limit exposure to pesticides and other contaminants.

Conventional farming methods, such as keeping livestock indoors and feeding them hormones, increase the size of livestock.

The term *sustainable agriculture* was first used in 1978 by Wes Jackson, an agricultural scientist, so it would seem to be a newer idea than organic farming. However, organic farming and sustainable farming share many of the same goals. Wendell Berry, a farmer who also wrote about sustainable farming, describes three important parts of sustainable farming: protecting ecosystems, protecting farm communities, and giving farmers a livelihood. According to Berry, if these three goals are met, farming methods will be lasting, or sustainable.

Organic and sustainable farming are part of a growing international recognition that humans must protect the environment to protect our own health and welfare. This protection involves preventing pollution, protecting wildlife, and conserving natural resources. The environmental movement gathered strength in the last half of the twentieth century, and organic and sustainable farming have become areas of interest along with it. Humans have farmed for centuries and continuously improved their methods. However, farming methods that are unsustainable and damage the soil are still common.

Two examples of environmental crises in the twentieth century show the relationship between concerns about the environment and agriculture. One example, known as the Dust Bowl, occurred in the 1930s in the United States. Farming methods in dry grasslands in the western United States and Canada removed deep-rooted grasses. Farmers also plowed fields, leaving the soil exposed. Several years of low rainfall dried the soil and prevented crops from growing. High winds began to blow the soil away. Farming became impossible, and hundreds of thousands of people were forced to move, especially from Texas and Oklahoma. Climates with low rainfall require special dry-land farming methods. If farmers in dry climates do not practice these methods, soil is damaged and the land becomes drier and impossible to farm. When farmers ignored the environment they were working in, there were devastating consequences.

The Dust Bowl of the 1930s was an environmental crisis that left fields barren and farms uninhabitable.

In 1962, marine biologist Rachel Carson wrote about the damage caused by pesticides to wildlife and humans in her book *Silent Spring*. She wrote about DDT, a pesticide that was widely used to kill mosquitos and pest insects on crops in the United States and around the world. DDT has few effects on humans, but it was found to remain in animal bodies for long periods of time. DDT was responsible for the near extinction of bald eagles because the high concentrations thinned the shells of the eagles' eggs, causing them to break before they hatched. Carson's book increased the growth of the environmental movement in the United States. Her arguments against using pesticides are a model for the arguments organic and sustainable farmers make for their methods.

After scientists proved that DDT put bald eagles in danger of extinction, the effects of that and other pesticides on the environment received more attention. This sparked the environmental movement in the United States.

# Officially Organic

Since most people buy their food in grocery stores and not from farmers, the only way to know if food is produced organically is by a method of certification. This means an expert must study the way a farm is run to make sure it uses only organic methods. If the farm passes, food and other products the farm makes can be labeled organic when they are sold. Beginning in the 1970s, various groups were formed in the United States to certify organic food, but it became clear that a single system was needed. In 1990, the US government passed the Organic Foods Production Act, and in 1997, the rules for what was organic were first published. They are based on a national list of substances prohibited in organic food.

The new rules created outrage in the organic food community because they allowed the use of several methods that most people considered nonorganic, including the use of some genetically modified organisms, or GMOs. GMOs are plants or animals that have had a gene from another organism added to their DNA to make them stronger or more productive. People have been researching harmful and helpful farming methods ever since, and the debate still continues.

# SUSTAINABLE AND ORGANIC FARMS

Organic and sustainable farmers grow and care for crops and animals differently than conventional farmers do. Organic farmers avoid adding artificial fertilizers to soil and using pesticides to kill weeds and pest animals. They also avoid planting the same crop over and over again in the same fields. Organic farming of animals emphasizes giving animals plenty of space, fresh air, and food, and not administering antibiotics or growth hormones.

## Fertilizers

Fertilizers contain nutrients that plants need to grow. When a field is planted year after year and the crops are taken away, nutrients are also taken away from the soil. Conventional farms often add nutrients every year by spreading artificial fertilizer on the soil. Most artificial fertilizers contain nitrogen, phosphorus, potassium, and small amounts of other minerals

Organically raised livestock are allowed to graze on grass in open pastures.

plants need. Another common source of artificial fertilizer is sewage sludge produced by sewage treatment plants because it contains nutrients and is inexpensive.

Artificial fertilizers require energy to produce, and they provide only some of the nutrients needed to make soils fertile. Treated sewage sludge is tested for contaminants, but it can still contain dangerous substances, including heavy metals. Heavy metals such as lead, cadmium, and chromium are poisonous and can build up in animals and humans. Regulation and monitoring ensures that sewage sludge is free of substances we know are harmful. Research continues to look for new substances, such as medicines, in treated sewage sludge that might pose a risk to humans.

Organic farmers keep their soils fertile by recycling nutrients as much as possible. Recycling nutrients means adding nutrients from resources found on or close to the farm rather than using artificial fertilizers. Livestock manure is a traditional source of nutrients for crop fields. Manure produced by local livestock contains nutrients from plants grown in the area, so spreading manure on the fields returns those same nutrients to the soil.

Manure also contains bacteria that give the soil the ability to form its own nutrients. It is important to allow the manure to compost before using it as a fertilizer because it frees up nutrients and makes it easier for plants to absorb them. When manure sits in large piles for a few months or seasons (depending on location and weather), bacteria and fungi break down matter in the manure. After composting, a manure pile is smaller and the nutrients are more concentrated.

A farmer spreads manure from local livestock. Those animals eat organic feed, so the farmer can also label this crop as organic.

Organic farmers use other methods to reduce the need for fertilizers. Crop rotation that includes legumes adds nitrogen to the soil. Planting a cover crop, which holds the soil in place when a field is left fallow, helps stop water from carrying nutrients out of the soil. Finally, keeping the unused parts of crop plants, such as cornstalks, in the field and allowing them to return to the soil recycles the nutrients they contain.

## COMPOSTING

If you garden or grow plants inside, composting can be a perfect way to return nutrients to your soil. Composting is easy because microbes do most of the work for you. You just need a place to do it, such as a corner of your yard, a simple container, and waste from your kitchen and yard. A compost pile needs both nitrogen-rich material, such as kitchen scraps (not including meat), and carbon-rich material, such as dead leaves. Grass clippings count as nitrogen rich, so don't overload it with these. If you live in a place where the trees drop their leaves in the fall, collect as many as you can in yard-waste bags and keep them to feed to the compost when needed.

You may find that your compost pile heats up when it gets going. That means the microbes are working hard to break things down and helping to kill weed seeds. Turn your compost pile over every week or so to spread air throughout the pile. Also add water if it dries out. After three months, start a second pile and let the first one finish working. In a couple of months, you will have deep brown nutritious soil to put on your garden or potted plants.

# Pesticides

Plants make many of their own chemicals to defend against damaging organisms, but pests can still reduce crop yield. Pesticides are artificial chemicals that kill organisms that damage or cause disease in crops and livestock. The pesticides used in the largest amounts kill weeds, which are plants that grow alongside crop plants and crowd out or take nutrients from the crops. These pesticides are called herbicides. They can prevent weed seeds from germinating, or beginning to grow.

Other pesticides kill roundworms and fungi, which attack and kill plants. However, pesticides can also kill beneficial microorganisms that improve the soil quality by freeing up nutrients for crops to use. They also kill different types of fungi and roundworms that prey on crop-eating insects.

Organic and sustainable farmers find other ways to get rid of pests. One of the ways they do this is by learning a pest's life cycle and interfering with it. Many pests attack only one kind of plant, so crop rotation is one way of interrupting a pest's life cycle. Pests that survive one year because the plant they eat is being grown have no food the next year when a different crop

Old world bollworms are one example of pests that damage crops.

is growing. Some plants can also make their own pest killers. In northern climates, planting rye grass after a corn harvest and then allowing the rye to decompose during the winter releases chemicals that prevent weeds from growing.

A second way to control pests organically is to introduce the pests to their own enemies. For example, some bacteria produce chemicals that starve caterpillars. These bacteria can be sprayed on plants to repel caterpillars without hurting the animals that later eat the plants.

Finally, planting different crops together can make it more difficult for pests to move from one plant to another. This method, known as push-pull, was developed by farmers growing corn in Africa. Between rows of corn, the farmers plant silverleaf desmodium, a plant that produces a natural insect repellent that pushes moths away from the corn. At the edges of the cornfield, they plant a second crop, Napier grass, which moths like, helping pull the moths away from the corn.

# Conventional Animals and Organic Animals

Conventional farmers also use a lot of chemicals when raising animals. Some of these chemicals add nutrients to animals' diets, and others add hormones and antibiotics to speed the animals' growth. Conventional farmers also use pesticides to prevent worm infections, insect parasites, and fungal infections in animals. And when animals get sick from bacterial infections, conventional farmers treat them with medicines.

Organic farmers must use other methods to raise healthy animals. Hormones and antibiotics are prohibited on organic farms because of

As part of the push-pull method, African farmers plant Napier grass on the edges of cornfields to draw moths away from the corn.

concern for the animals' welfare and for human health. Instead, organic livestock are fed nutrient-rich organic food. Organic farmers also do their best to keep animals disease free so that they will not need medicines. Keeping a clean farm and controlling parasites by interrupting their life cycles reduces infection. If livestock do become ill, they must be treated, but if they are treated with a prohibited medicine, their meat cannot be sold as organic.

There are also rules about how organic livestock must be fed and treated. They must be allowed to be outside when the weather permits. They must eat organic feeds and be able to graze on land that has not been treated with pesticides or artificial fertilizers. Pasture grazing also improves

# ANTIBIOTICS

Antibiotics control bacterial infections in humans and animals. But they are sometimes used too much, or used in nonmedical situations. One nonmedical use is administering them to cattle and other farm animals in their feed throughout their lives. Scientists have found that farm animals given antibiotics have higher growth rates than cattle that are not given antibiotics. This means that farmers can sell their livestock more quickly and for more money. However, the overuse of antibiotics and their use in nonmedical situations has caused many antibiotic-resistant bacteria to evolve. This process works in the same way that pesticide resistance occurs in insects and other crop pests.

an animal's health. Animals must have access to sunlight and shade as they need it, clean water, and clean bedding materials. They must also have enough space for exercise. These rules are required by law for meat from livestock to be labeled as organic. The farm must also have passed a certification process to be called organic, and rules are enforced by regular inspections.

# Genetically Modified Organisms

Another way organic farmers' practices set them apart is the prohibition of GMOs. Humans have been modifying the genes of plants and animals for centuries by selective breeding. To do this, breeders choose offspring that have traits they desire and allows only those offspring to mate. The desired trait is then more common in the offspring of those pairs. All of our crops

To be considered organic, sheep, cattle, and goats must be able to graze in pastures for at least 120 days of the year.

and livestock have been enhanced by selective breeding. But GMOs are different because their DNA is modified by genetic engineering methods. Usually the goal of the method is to combine traits from organisms that cannot breed together. Genetic engineering uses laboratory methods to move genes between organisms without breeding.

In the United States, organic foods cannot contain GMOs. Examples of GMOs include crops that are resistant to certain herbicides and plants that have been given genes from bacteria that protect them against caterpillars. GMOs have also been developed to be more nutritious. Golden rice is a genetically modified rice plant that was given the ability to form vitamin

A in the rice kernel. The rice is intended to prevent vitamin A deficiency, a serious health problem in many countries.

Some genetically modified crops, such as golden rice, were developed only with human nutrition in mind. Others, such as pesticide-resistant crops, are made by crop companies or pesticide companies and can only be purchased directly from the company. They promise increased crop

This sweet corn has been genetically modified to resist herbicides and insect pests. Debate continues on whether these changes could cause problems for people who eat the corn.

productivity, but similar to other manufactured products, their main purpose is to create profit for the company. Sometime this comes at the expense of traditional farming methods. For example, many genetically modified crops are sold with an agreement that farmers will not keep seed to plant the following year. Instead, they must buy more seed from the company. Farmers have been sued for trying to keep the seed of genetically modified crops. This is another example of unsustainable farming, using expensive outside materials instead of recycling materials, such as crop seeds, that are produced on the farm.

Animals have also been genetically modified. For example, cows have been genetically engineered to produce milk with the same proteins as human milk. Some of these GMO livestock have been bred for research into new medicines or human diseases. However, genetically modified livestock animals are not raised outside of experimental farms, and their products are not available for sale.

# Organic Certification

To be sold as organic, foods must be grown, prepared, and handled according to certain regulations. Nearly ninety countries across the globe now have official regulations that define what can be called organic and what cannot.

The US Department of Agriculture (USDA) has certified more than 25,000 farms and processing facilities as organic. Most of these are in the United States, but some are located outside the country. Land that produces organic food must not have been treated with any nonorganic substances for three years. The farm must submit a history of the land

## Case In POINT

# THE ENVIROPIG™

Genetically modified crops are now relatively common. Less common are genetically modified animals. The Enviropig™ is an animal created partly for research in 1999 by scientists at the University of Guelph in Canada. The pig has a gene that causes it to produce an enzyme in its saliva and stomach. When the pig eats grain, the enzyme releases phosphorus in the feed that a normal pig cannot produce. This has two effects. First, the pig gets more nutrition from the grain it eats, so it needs to be fed fewer mineral or enzyme supplements. Second, the pig produces waste with less phosphorus, which can pollute waterways.

The Enviropig was developed to solve an environmental problem and to create a pig that costs less to raise. Critics argue that the better solution is to change the way pigs are raised so they are not so concentrated in one place, reducing their environmental effects.

The process to allow Enviropigs to be used as farm animals is a long one. In 2012, the industry group that paid for the Enviropig research at the University of Guelph stopped providing funding. There are presently no Enviropigs in existence, and the research has stopped, although their genetic material has been kept.

and methods used, as well as a farm plan. This information is given to a certification agent, who makes the decision about whether the farm is organic. Once the certifying agent certifies the farm, the products the farm produces can be called organic.

When a farm is certified, it is allowed to display the USDA's organic seal on its products. The seal means that crops were grown without pesticides, artificial fertilizers, or sewage sludge and do not contain GMOs. It means that meat comes from animals that were not fed antibiotics, growth hormones, or feeds that were nonorganic.

## Local Food

A grocery store in almost any city or town will carry fruit, vegetables, and meat from hundreds of miles away. Sometimes products might come from thousands of miles away. In the United States, foods from Europe, Asia, South America, Australia, and New Zealand are easily available. This is also

The USDA Organic seal ensures that produce, dairy, or meat products were raised and produced organically.

true in many other countries throughout the world. This is only possible by burning energy to transport the food in jets, trucks, and ships. One part of sustainable agriculture is the idea that local food is better for the environment, for farmers, and for the people who eat the food.

Most fruits and vegetables have labels that easily identify whether it is organic and what country the food came from. It can be more difficult to know where food came from within a country. One solution to this dilemma is to buy groceries at a local farmers' market. At most farmers' markets, local farmers sell their produce directly, so the buyer knows it comes from nearby. The buyer can ask the farmer how the food was produced. Shipping and selling products locally also keeps money in the community. The farmers don't have to pay for transportation or packaging, so they receive more income. Consumers can save money for the same reasons. Thinking about whether the food you buy is good for you, good for the farmer, and

## Case In POINT
# CERTIFIED SUSTAINABLE FARMING

Farmers can practice sustainable farming without practicing organic farming. There is no legal certification for sustainable farming. However, there are independent sustainable certification organizations. The Food Alliance has a certification system for sustainable farming that includes many of the same requirements as those for organic foods. It also considers the effects of the farm on wildlife habitat and farmworkers. The Food Alliance has certified more than 330 farms and ranches in North America.

When you visit your local farmers' market, you can get to know the people who grow your food.

good for the community and environment (as well as any animals involved

in production) is at the heart of eating organic.

# BENEFITS OF ORGANIC AND SUSTAINABLE AGRICULTURE

Organic and sustainable farming methods bring environmental, health, and financial benefits to those involved. These methods reduce pollution in the form of nutrients and toxins that kill plants and animals. They also use less energy, which means less pollution from burning fossil fuels. They emphasize the preservation of natural biodiversity by growing a variety of plants. Organic and sustainable farming methods are better for human health because they avoid the use of toxic compounds, which can find their way into foods or harm those working or living around farms. The financial benefits include improved incomes and better working conditions for farmers, farmworkers, and other workers in the many steps food takes to get from the farm to our tables.

Organic and sustainable agriculture benefits the lives of the farmers and consumers who buy the organic produce.

# Reducing Pollution

One of the greatest environmental benefits of organic and sustainable farming is the reduction of pollution. Artificial fertilizers are added to the soil in crop fields, but they do not always stay there. Since the chemicals in fertilizers dissolve in water, runoff filled with fertilizers finds its way to streams, rivers, lakes, and finally the ocean. Some water seeps deep into the ground and becomes groundwater. Groundwater is used for irrigation, or the watering of farm soil, but it is also used as drinking water in many places. High levels of nitrogen from fertilizers are especially dangerous for infants and children who drink the water.

When the nitrogen and phosphorus in fertilizers enter rivers, lakes, and oceans, they feed the algae living there. When fertilizers are added, the algae can grow and reproduce without control. Usually the algae themselves do not hurt anything. But the algae die and sink to the bottom of the lake or ocean. On the bottom, bacteria eat the dead algae. Bacteria use oxygen when they grow. When a lot of algae die, it can cause a population explosion in bacteria. The bacteria then remove all the oxygen from the water near the bottom of the lake or ocean, making it impossible for other organisms to live there.

Each year there is a large area of the Gulf of Mexico near the mouth of the Mississippi River that becomes a "dead zone." Artificial fertilizers washed from fields into the water of the Mississippi enter the Gulf of Mexico. The bacteria use up oxygen by feeding on dead algae, making that part of the Gulf a suffocating trap for anything that needs oxygen. The organisms affected include fish, shrimp, and turtles. The dead zone threatens fisheries and the plants and animals of the Gulf. All around the world, similar dead zones form in lakes and oceans because of artificial fertilizers.

Organic and sustainable farms work to use natural methods of fertilization to avoid this runoff. The nitrogen and phosphorus in manure, compost, or decaying plants are released more slowly than the nutrients

After rains, fertilizer in fields runs off into nearby bodies of water.

Algae blooms, resulting from high amounts of fertilizer runoff, make it impossible for many water species to survive.

in artificial fertilizers. This allows crops to take up more nutrients and reduces the amount that is carried away by water. Studies show that organic farming and sustainable agriculture methods reduce the amount of nutrients leaving the farm's soils, often by one-half or more, preventing harm to the environment.

Rotating crops can also prevent soil erosion. For example, planting winter rye in the fall stops wind and water from carrying soil away from harvested fields that would otherwise be bare. Soil loss can hurt a farm's ability to grow crops. The soil also clogs rivers and lakes. Soil forms silt in rivers and lakes, which can stop sunlight from reaching plants and algae and suffocate plants and animals when it settles.

Without plant roots to hold it together and leaves to shield it from rain, this exposed soil has started to erode. Crop rotation can stop this process.

# Reducing Resistance and Creating Healthier Ecosystems

Many farmers use pesticides to kill pests and disease organisms. However, there are always a few organisms that are resistant to a pesticide. They have a gene or combination of genes that allows them to survive the pesticide.

Once the pesticide is gone, these few survivors have no competition from other members of their species and can reproduce rapidly. In this way, using the same pesticide year after year soon creates pests that are no longer killed by the pesticide. At that point, a new pesticide must be invented and applied. Replacing pesticides with new ones costs a lot of money and lost crops.

Pesticides also kill bugs and animals they were not intended to harm. Some of the insects killed are considered beneficial because they provide a valuable service to a farm ecosystem. Pesticides also rarely stay only where

## To Your
## HEALTH

## HUMAN HEALTH

If used appropriately, most pesticides are rated as safe for humans by the US Environmental Protection Agency. But millions of people still get sick and thousands die each year around the world from accidental overdoses of pesticides. Usually these are farmworkers or individuals who were unaware of the risk. In many cases, the long-term effects of chemicals are unknown and difficult to discover, but there is evidence that they may affect wildlife and humans in some cases. Because organic farming does not use pesticides, farmworkers and consumers are not at risk from poisoning.

# PLANTING A GARDEN

Want to know what it's like to be an organic farmer without buying a farm? Start your own organic garden!

- A garden does not have to be planted on a plot of land. If you have limited space, you can plant your garden in containers, such as pots or recycled containers. If you are using containers, make sure they are wide and deep enough to fit the plants you are growing. Tomatoes need big pots, while smaller plants such as peas or lettuce need smaller ones.

- Timing is important for farming and gardening, so do some research on what grows best where you live and start the seeds or seedlings at the right time of the year.

- Prepare your soil by turning it to loosen it if you are planting in the ground. If you are using containers, make sure the soil has good drainage and a good combination of mineral and decaying organic matter. Adding compost can increase the organic material in the soil.

- Most vegetables need lots of sunlight to produce, so locate your garden or place your containers in a sunny place outside. If you grow inside, put your plants in a bright window or on a well-lit balcony.

- Make sure your plants are watered enough (but not too much) and then just let them grow.

- Support your plants with stakes or strings if necessary, and harvest them when they are ready.

they're sprayed. When they are washed away with water, they enter the ecosystem around the farm.

Organic farming and sustainable agriculture use natural methods to prevent and discourage the growth of pests and diseases. These methods include interrupting pest life cycles with crop rotation and planting mixed-crop fields to interfere with pest movements. Because of this, pests do not become resistant, and there is no cost for new pesticides or lost

An organic farmer hand-picks pests from his crops. This organic form of pest control takes a lot of time and effort.

# TASTE TEST

Many people claim organic foods taste better than the same foods grown using conventional farming methods. Everyone has different tastes, but why not put some foods to the test? For your taste test, find organic and nonorganic fruits or vegetables that are as similar as possible. For example, compare the same varieties of apples. Once you have decided what you will test, buy one of each. Make sure to keep them separate. Then decide who will conduct the experiment and who else will taste test with you. The person conducting the experiment will be the only one who knows which apple is organic and which is not. After the conductor slices each apple, try a sample of each. Which one do you prefer? Can you detect any differences?

crops and animals. One other benefit of not using pesticides is that the organisms that eat and kill our pests, helping our crops and soil, remain unharmed. Communities also benefit when farmers spend less money on buying outside materials, such as pesticides and herbicide-resistant seeds, promoting sustainable living. And consumers benefit as well, knowing their produce is grown organically and sustainably.

# CHALLENGES OF ORGANIC FARMING

**M**any people agree that sustainable and organic farming practices safer, healthier methods than conventional farming. Yet there are concerns about organic and sustainable farming that make them difficult for some to accept. One of the main challenges of these farming methods is the cost.

## Cost

Most organic foods are more expensive than foods produced by conventional farming. There are several reasons for this. Organic foods are less common, so they are in demand. Prices are naturally high for anything that people want that is in limited supply. Most organic farms are smaller than conventional farms, and because of this it costs more to produce each item of food. During handling and transportation, organic foods must be kept separate from nonorganic foods to ensure they are not accidentally

Many shoppers will pay more for organic produce because they think it's healthier or tastes better, or because it is better for the environment.

## COMPARE PRICES AND PRODUCTS

Just how much more do organic products cost than conventional products? Visit your local grocery store and compare the prices for similar kinds of produce that are organic and nonorganic. Select a few examples, such as vegetables, fruits, and meats if they are available. Make sure you convert the prices per amount to units that can be compared, such as dollars per pound. Compare the price differences. Are all organic products more expensive than their conventional counterparts? If you have a local farmers' market, compare prices there. Are local products more or less expensive than similar products in the grocery store? Finally, if you are able, consider revisiting the grocery store at a later time to see if prices have changed in a different season for different kinds of produce.

combined. Because organic foods are produced in smaller quantities, it costs more to transport and process them than it does for large quantities of conventionally farmed products.

Raising livestock for meat under organic animal treatment guidelines is also more expensive than caring for livestock at a conventional farm. But many people are willing to accept the added cost because they value animal welfare.

## Slim Pickings

Practicing sustainability means eating locally, or eating what's in season where you live. That can shrink the number of food choices. In the United States, consumers are used to being able to buy strawberries almost year round. But strawberries only grow in the summer in most of the United

States. Many of the fresh fruits and vegetables Americans are used to eating during the winter months in northern climates would be unavailable if we only ate locally produced foods. Instead, northerners would be eating more

Many people are willing to pay higher prices for organic foods.

# A NEED FOR RESEARCH

Some critics of organic and sustainable agriculture have said that the amount of food we need to feed the human population cannot be produced by sustainable and organic agriculture. Some studies show that organic farming produces similar yields to conventional farming and others show that it does not. Far less research has been done to understand organic and sustainable farming. More study is needed to determine which sustainable farming methods are best.

preserved vegetables and produce that can be stored through the winter, such as squash, apples, and root vegetables.

Eating local foods also means not eating foods that come from very distant places. In the United States, this means bananas, pineapples, and other tropical fruits that we're used to eating all year. Could you live without these fruits? Could you live without fresh tomatoes in the middle of winter? While this may seem like a disadvantage of supporting organic and sustainable farming, it's important to consider the cost to the environment and our local communities when we make these choices. Even though eating organically can mean higher prices and fewer selections at times, the organic movement is on the rise.

# FOOD DESERTS

The USDA defines a food desert as a part of the country where fresh fruit, vegetables, and whole foods are not available. The lack of availability can be because there are not grocery stores or markets, or because the people who live there cannot easily get to the stores that do exist. Mari Gallagher, an independent food researcher, first identified food deserts in Chicago, Illinois. In many neighborhoods in Chicago's South Side, residents cannot easily get to a grocery store that carries fresh and whole foods, and local corner stores do not carry them.

First Lady Michelle Obama's Lets' Move! program includes a plan to improve access to healthy and affordable food in food deserts. The plan will help grocery stores and smaller stores obtain fresh foods. Other solutions include local government assistance to grocery stores wishing to operate in food desert areas, encouraging farmers' markets in food desert areas, encouraging stores that do not carry food (such as drugstores) to add fresh foods to their inventories, and creating community gardens.

# FUTURE OF ORGANIC FOODS

**B**etween 2004 and 2011, organic food sales increased from $11 billion to $25 billion in the United States. Between 2000 and 2011, the amount of land being farmed organically tripled in the United States, although it is still only approximately 1 percent of farmland. Approximately half of Americans prefer to eat organic food rather than food grown on conventional farms, making the demand for organic food in the United States larger than the amount of food available for consumers. Because of this, the use of organic and sustainable farming methods is expected to continue to grow in the United States.

## Growth in Other Countries

In other parts of the world, the growth of organic and sustainable farming is just as impressive and sometimes even more widespread. Between 1999 and 2012, the amount of land devoted to organic farming in the world tripled.

More and more grocery stores are helping bring organic foods to consumers. In 2015, Whole Foods Market announced a plan to triple the number of its stores in the United States.

The largest consumer of certified organic food is the United States, with Europe following close behind. Many countries with large areas of land devoted to organic farming are producing food for export to these consumer countries. This is especially true of Latin American countries, which are producing organic meats, coffee, and sugarcane.

Some of these products compete with US products, and growers in the United States will have to adapt to the international market. This means carefully choosing crops and livestock that can be grown best in the conditions of the United States, which includes higher standards of living and costs for farm labor. It will also mean developing farming and distribution methods that allow farmers in the United States to sell their organic products at more places than the local farmers' market. Making farms and distribution systems larger will also be a challenge to keeping the standards of organic and sustainable farming.

## Adopting Organic Practices

The ideas of sustainable farming—such as reducing expensive and damaging artificial fertilizers and pesticides and protecting the soil—have changed how conventional farmers and farm researchers work. The goal of the Green Revolution was to increase yields. But many scientists and farmers have come to believe that caring only about yields may threaten land and health in the future. Many conventional farmers are reducing their use of fertilizers and pesticides while not becoming completely organic.

Many farmers are also using methods such as crop rotation to protect the soil and reduce fertilizer and pesticide use. These methods also reduce the use of machines, which decreases the amount of fossil fuels being burned. They also protect the soil on the farm and the environment around the farm from runoff.

This farm in Wisconsin alternates soybean and corn crops to protect against erosion and soil depletion.

While these types of farms cannot be certified organic, they are a step in the organic direction. Gordon Conway, a professor of international development, has called this approach "the doubly green revolution." He says, "We require . . . a revolution that is even more productive than the first Green Revolution, even more 'Green' in terms of conserving natural resources and the environment, and even more effective in reducing

## Case In POINT

# POLLINATORS AND ECOSYSTEM SERVICES

One of the goals of sustainable farming that will continue into the future is to prevent damage to ecosystem services. Ecosystem services are work that the natural environment does that helps humans and other living things survive. Pollinators are an example of an ecosystem service. Many crops need an insect pollinator, such as a honeybee, to produce the fruit. The pollinator takes pollen from one plant to the flower of a second plant. This fertilizes the plant's eggs, allowing it to grow fruit. In return for this work, the plant provides the pollinator with a rich sugar solution called nectar.

Since many pollinators are insects, they are killed by the same pesticides that are used to kill insects considered pests. Many crops are pollinated by honeybees that are kept by beekeepers and transported to fields for a time to pollinate a crop. However, honeybee populations have been in decline for several years, and there is a fear that losing this ecosystem service may threaten some crops. The cause of the decline may be the result of a combination of factors, including disease, climate change, and pesticides.

hunger and poverty." Conway believes these changes will require the use of genetically modified crops and careful use of pesticides and fertilizers, which organic farmers are strongly against. However, it is likely that conventional farming will change in the future in response to ideas and methods coming from organic and sustainable farming.

The future of sustainable and organic farming looks bright. Demand for organic products remains strong, and more people are becoming aware of the risks of conventional farming and the benefits of sustainable methods.

# BIO-CHAR COMPOSTS

Scientists working in the Amazon tropical lowlands, which usually have poor soils, have found some very rich soils called *terra preta*, or black earth. They believe that centuries ago local people added charcoal, or partly burned woody matter, to these soils. The charcoal, or bio-char as it is sometimes called, is responsible for the richness of these soils. Bio-char has become a subject of research to understand how it holds and increases the amount of nutrients in soil. It seems to have something to do with the carbon and the microorganisms that are able to live in the bio-char. It is also possible that bio-char may be a way to fight climate change by keeping more carbon in the soil rather than allowing it to become a greenhouse gas in the atmosphere. Human-caused climate change is occurring because we burn fossil fuels and cut down forests, releasing carbon dioxide into the atmosphere. The carbon dioxide traps the sun's radiation in the atmosphere, causing a rapid warming of the planet. To prevent climate change, we will need to find ways to store more carbon outside of the atmosphere.

Bio-char composts are now available for use and can be easily made by slowly burning waste wood so that it forms charcoal rather than ashes. This method could also revolutionize how we compost soil outside of the Amazon basin. Understanding ancient agricultural methods and discovering new methods will be an important part of moving to more organic and sustainable farming in the future.

Organic farmers, such as this one, benefit from organic and sustainable practices because they know where their food is coming from, and they know it is healthy for themselves, the animals, the land, and the environment.

The more we think about eating healthy, responsibly, and with care for our communities and environment, the more sustainable our food can be. Taking part in the organic and sustainable movement allows farmers, consumers, and communities to live healthfully and sustainably.

# Working as an
# ORGANIC FARMER

The duties of an organic farmer depend on the kind of food the farmer produces. And since all growing things have a life cycle, the farmer's tasks also depend on the season. As Australian organic farmer Alasdair Smithson says, "One of the great things about organic farming is that no two days are the same, which makes it a good profession for those of us who like variety and thinking on our feet."

Organic farmers, like all farmers, start their day before dawn. On a dairy farm, the first task is to set out feed for the cows and bring the cattle into the barn for milking. This involves getting each cow into her stall, washing her udders, and attaching the milking machines. Once the milking is done, the manure the cows have left needs to be shoveled up and carted out. Then the cows are led back to the pasture to feed.

On a vegetable farm, the cool morning is best spent hand weeding a field of vegetables and getting the weeds onto the compost pile. The farmer walks through other crop fields to look for pest damage and to see how close the crop is to harvest. The afternoon may be spent harvesting a crop to be sent to a local food distributor or local restaurants. The harvested plants must be washed and then packaged for transportation. In the evening, the farmer will complete a log of the day's activities as a requirement for organic certification. There will also be business e-mails to return and paperwork to prepare.

# GLOSSARY

**antibiotic:** a chemical that treats and prevents disease and is also commonly given to animals in their feed or water to increase growth rates

**conventional farming:** farming that may use artificial fertilizers, pesticides, genetically modified organisms, antibiotics, growth hormones, and crowded conditions for animals to improve crop and livestock yields

**ecosystem:** a collection of nonliving materials and living organisms that interact with each other

**microorganism:** an extremely small living thing visible only with a microscope

**organic farming:** farming without the use of artificial fertilizers, pesticides, genetically modified organisms, and unnecessary drugs, while treating animals humanely

**pesticide:** a chemical that is used to kill pests of crops and animals such as weeds, insects, nematodes, and fungi

**sustainable farming:** farming with methods that maintain soil quality, cycle nutrients, limit damage to ecosystems, provide farm livelihoods, and maintain local communities

**yield:** a measure of how much a crop produces per area of land that is planted, such as bushels per acre

# SOURCE NOTES

**56.** Gordon Conway, *One Billion Hungry: Can We Feed The World?* (New York: Comstock Publishing Associates, 2012).

**60.** "A Day in the Life of an Organic Vegetable Farmer," *Australian Organic*, July 31, 2014, http://blog.munchcrunchorganics.com.au/a-day-in-the-life-of-an-organic-vegetable-farmer-published-by-australian-organic/.

# SELECTED BIBLIOGRAPHY

Conway, Gordon. *One Billion Hungry: Can We Feed The World?* New York: Comstock Publishing Associates, 2012.

Corselius, K., M. Wisniewski and M. Ritchie. "Sustainable Agriculture: Making Money, Making Sense." *The Institute for Agriculture and Trade Policy*, March 2001. http://www.iatp.org/files/Sustainable_Agriculture_-_ Making_Money_Making_.pdf.

Hansen, Anne Larkin. *The Organic Farming Manual: A Comprehensive Guide to Starting and Running a Certified Organic Farm*. North Adams, MA: Storey Publishing, 2010.

"Organic Agriculture." *United States Department of Agriculture*, April 25, 2015. http://www.ers.usda.gov/topics/natural-resources-environment/ organic-agriculture.aspx.

Solbrig, Otto Thomas. *So Shall You Reap: Farming and Crops in Human Affairs*. Washington, DC: Island Press, 1994.

# FURTHER INFORMATION

Ballard, Carol. *Sustainable Farming*. Mankato, MN: Arcturus Publishing, 2009. Read more about the need for, history, and methods of sustainable farming.

LocalHarvest
http://www.localharvest.org/organic-farms/visiting.html
This site will help you find an organic farm near you to visit.

Organic.org
http://www.organic.org/kids
This site has great resources and games for learning about organic farming.

Perdew, Laura. *Eating Local*. Minneapolis, MN: Lerner, 2016. Read about the ways in which you can eat local, and why it's important to do so.

Roberts, Jack L. *Organic Agriculture: Protecting Our Food Supply or Chasing Imaginary Risks?* Minneapolis, MN: Twenty-First Century Books, 2012. Learn more about the roots of organic agriculture, the debate about factory farms, and GMOs.

USDA for Kids
http://www.usda.gov/wps/portal/usda/usdahome?navid=FOR_KIDS
The USDA offers resources about agriculture and other topics on this site.

Vogel, Julia. *Save the Planet: Local Farms and Sustainable Foods*. Ann Arbor, MI: Cherry Lake Publishing, 2010. Read more about sustainable farming and some of its challenges.

# INDEX

## Photo Acknowledgments

The images in this book are used with the permission of: © panco971/Shutterstock Images, p. 1; © Annette Shaff/Shutterstock Images, p. 5; © The Yorck Project, p. 7; © vesnushka/Shutterstock Images, p. 9; © pokku/Shutterstock Images, p. 12; © Esdelval/iStockphoto, p. 13; © branislavpudar/Shutterstock Images, p. 15; © Everett Historical/Shutterstock Images, p. 17; © Al Mueller/Shutterstock Images, p. 18; © Lya Cattel/iStockphoto, p. 21; © Lisa S./Shutterstock Images, p. 23; © Madlen/Shutterstock Images, p. 24; © AFNR/Shutterstock Images, p. 25; © Thana Nattribhop/Shutterstock Images, p. 27; © Alessandro Zocc/Shutterstock Images, p. 29; © chanwangrong/Shutterstock Images, p. 30; © Francis Joseph Dean/Deanpictures/Newscom, p. 33; © lilly3/iStockphoto, p. 35; © Fuse/Thinkstock, p. 37; © Brent Stirton/Getty Images/Thinkstock, p. 39; © Jessica Bethke/Shutterstock Images, p. 40; © Vladimir Salman/Shutterstock Images, p. 41; © Monique Rodriguez/iStockphoto, p. 43; © Matthias G. Ziegler/Shutterstock Images, p. 44; © Greg Gibson/AP Images, p. 47; © Danielle Balderas/Shutterstock Images, p. 49; © Bruce Leighty/Getty Images, p. 51; © LPETTET/iStockphoto, p. 53; © Earl D. Walker/Shutterstock Images, p. 55; © Claudio Divizia/Shutterstock Images, p. 58; © Andresr/Shutterstock Images, p. 59.

Front Cover: © iStockphoto.com/sndr (top left); © iStockphoto.com/carterdayne (top right); © panco971/Shutterstock.com (bottom left); © Mint Images/Helen Norman/Getty Images (bottom right).